MATH ADVANTAGE

PARENT PREVIEW

This brochure provides information that will help your child achieve success using Math Advantage.

Now your child is ready to build the basics upon which future success in math depends. You know this is an important year, but it's hard to help unless you know what your child is learning. This brochure is a preview of

- what your child will be learning in math this year,
- some of the vocabulary words that are important to know,
- and a few activities to do throughout the year that will be fun as well as good practice.

The **Math Advantage** program also provides help in other ways. The **Home Note**, located at the bottom of every lesson, tells how to review with your child the work that was done in school. You can use the **Home Note** to ask your child about that day's math lesson.

Throughout the year you will receive the **School-Home Connection** page. This will be sent to you at the beginning of every chapter. The **School-Home Connection** tells about

- the specific math concepts and vocabulary that your child will be learning,
- and additional activities to do at home that will provide extra practice.

By keeping these letters in a folder, you can help your child review and improve math skills all year long.

At the end of each chapter in your child's math book is a page called *Math Fun*. This game or activity is a delightful way to practice the skills just learned.

"Why do I have to learn this?"

This is the question both parents and teachers hear from students. You can give your child a better understanding of how math is used in real life by sharing with them how you use math every day.

Point out how you use math to

- measure ingredients in a recipe.
- sort coins needed for toll roads.
- decide on the size of container you need for storing leftovers.
- keep track of dates on a calendar.
- sort clothes, foods, and utensils.
- schedule times for each family member's activities.

Talking with your child about these routine events in life can lead to all kinds of exciting conversations. By sharing the value of math in this casual way, your child will also value what he or she is learning about math every day.

Local, State, and National Goals

The instruction and math content in **Math Advantage** is presented in a way designed to develop these local, state, and national goals. Students should

1. learn to value mathematics.
2. become confident in their ability to do mathematics.
3. become mathematical problem solvers.
4. learn to communicate mathematically.
5. learn to reason mathematically.

Students achieve these goals by learning the skills, following a thinking process, and using a variety of strategies to solve problems.

Lessons in this math book will present problems for your child to solve. Your child's teacher will use the plan, shown below, to guide your child to a solution. Help your child use this process by giving prompts for thinking about and solving a problem that needs to be solved at home.

Understand the Problem

Plan How to Solve It

Solve It

Look Back and Check Your Work

What Your Child Will Learn This Year

The core skills and some of the words that are developed in **Math Advantage** during this year are listed in the table below. Look for these words in the Picture Glossary, located at the back of your child's math book.

CORE SKILLS	VOCABULARY WORDS
act out addition and subtraction sentences	*addition sentence, subtraction sentence*
learn addition and subtraction facts to 10	*add, subtract, equals*
identify and sort shapes	*cone, cube, cylinder, pyramid, sphere, rectangle, square, triangle, circle*
learn ways to find sums and differences through 18	*doubles, doubles plus one, doubles minus one, count on, count back*
recognize how addition and subtraction are related	*fact family*
understand numbers and place value through 100	*tens, ones*
compare and order numbers through 100	*greater, less, before, after, between*
tell time and use a calendar	*hour, half hour, o'clock*
use a ruler to measure length	*ruler, inch, centimeter*
use special tools to measure weight, capacity, and temperature	*balance, heavier, lighter, weight*
show and name simple fractions	*fractions, half, third, fourth*
read simple tables and graphs	*bar graph, picture graph, tally marks*
add and subtract two-digit numbers	*sum, difference*

ACTIVITIES

Introduce these activities when you know your child has studied the content. Repeat the activities throughout the year so that you can help your child review and improve their math skills.

Pictures of Tens and Ones

In this activity, children draw pictures to show tens and ones as they make their own models for numbers.

What you need: paper and crayons

What you do:

1. Ask your child to think of his or her own pictures to show tens and ones. Your child might, for example, draw trees to show tens and apples to show ones.

2. Have your child draw pictures to show numbers such as 15, 32, and 70.

3. Ask your child to draw a picture of another number for you to read.

4. Your child might like to make up a story to go with the numbers he or she has drawn.

· ·

Heads 'n' Tails Toss

This fun game focuses on basic addition and subtraction facts.

What you need: 10 pennies

What you do:

1. Have your child count as you place 10 pennies in his or her hand.

2. Ask your child to toss the pennies on a table and sort them according to whether heads or tails are shown.

3. Ask your child to say an addition sentence telling about the heads and tails. For example, 10 pennies that land 3 heads up and 7 tails up make the facts 3 + 7 = 10 or 7 + 3 = 10.

4. You can vary the game by having your child name the entire fact family that corresponds to the heads up and tails up pennies. For 3 heads up and 7 tails up, you might write the child's number sentences: 3 + 7 = 10, 7 + 3 = 10, 10 − 3 = 7, and 10 − 7 = 3.

Nickels and Pennies

This game teaches a variety of concepts, including identifying the values of coins and counting coin collections.

What you need: 10 nickels and 10 pennies per player, 2 number cubes

How to play:

1. Have your child sort all the nickels and pennies into two piles. All coins should be placed between the players, in the "bank".

2. Set a goal amount, such as 20¢. Each player rolls the number cube and gets the number of pennies shown on the number cube from the bank.

3. When a player has 5 pennies, he or she trades them in at the bank for 1 nickel.

4. The first player to trade in enough pennies to have 20¢ (4 nickels) wins the round.

5. You can play more rounds of Nickels for Pennies with a new goal amount, such as 25¢ or 30¢.

6. When your child knows the value of a dime, you may use dimes and pennies to play the game for total amounts of 60¢ or 90¢.

Fraction Find

In this activity, it is important that children understand the meaning of fractions. This activity reinforces the meaning of the top and bottom numbers of a fraction and how they relate to one another.

What you need: no materials needed

What you do:

1. Help your child find examples of halves around your home.

2. For each example, ask your child questions such as, **"How many parts in the whole sandwich?"** (2) **"What part of the sandwich is each piece?"** (1 out of 2 or one half.)

3. When children seem comfortable with the concept of half, you may wish to work with fourths. Unfold a kitchen napkin and place a nut or bean on one section. Again, ask questions such as: **"How many parts does the napkin have?"** (4 parts) **"How many parts of the napkin have a bean on it?"** (1 part) **"What part of the napkin has a bean on it?"** (1 out of 4 parts, or 1/4 of the whole napkin.)

4. Continue to find other examples of fractions around the house. It is not necessary to write the fractions at this time; talking about the meaning of one half and one fourth is the most important thing.

Internet Activities

You can access additional math activities on the Harcourt Brace Home Page. The address is **http://www.hbschool.com**

Math
ADVANTAGE

HARCOURT
BRACE

ISBN 0-15-311140-2

90000 >

9 780153 111402

Printed in the United States of America

ISBN 0-15-311140-2

2 3 4 5 6 7 8 9 10 060 2000 99

Math
ADVANTAGE

School-Home Connection

HARCOURT
BRACE